The Death of Porn Study Guide

The Death of Porn
Study Guide

Men of Integrity Building a
World of Nobility

Ray Ortlund

CROSSWAY®
WHEATON, ILLINOIS

Contents

PART 1   REINTRODUCING THE CHARACTERS

Letter 1   *You Are Royalty*   3

Letter 2   *She Is Royalty*   9

Letter 3   *He Is Royalty*   15

PART 2   REIMAGINING THE FUTURE

Letter 4   *We Can Do This*   23

Letter 5   *We Can Work Together*   29

Letter 6   *We Can Make a World of Difference*   35

PART 1

———

REINTRODUCING THE CHARACTERS

You Are Royalty

Chapter Summary

You matter more than you know. You have God-given dignity that can make you fully alive and empower you to change the future. Here's your true identity: *you are royalty*. God the King created you in his image to represent him in the world. This is why even from childhood we all have a sense of destiny—we all long to fulfill some big, bold, and noble purpose. This is what we can recover—that God created us for a purpose of greatness in our generation.

Our problem is not that we need more religion, more effort at being nicer, or more success at fulfilling our dreams. Our problem is that we have trivialized God, and then we have trivialized our own God-created selves. We are royal, but we are now also evil. We need to be re-created in God's image all over again. We change not by a religious try-harder mentality but only through the grace of Jesus. Jesus lived the faithful life we fail to live and died the shameful death we deserve to die, in order to bring us the forgiveness and renewal we need. The cross shows us that God is welcoming us out of hiding to receive mercy. We take two steps in response: believe that Jesus considers us worth fighting for, and prepare for battle.

Texts for Meditation and Memorization

Psalm 8:3–5

> When I look at your heavens, the work of your fingers,
>> the moon and the stars, which you have set in place,
> what is man that you are mindful of him,
>> and the son of man that you care for him?
>
> Yet you have made him a little lower than the heavenly beings
>> and crowned him with glory and honor.

2 Corinthians 5:17

> Therefore, if anyone is in Christ, he is a new creation. The old has passed away; behold, the new has come.

———

Questions for Reflection and Discussion

1. As you read the first letter, what one insight stood out to you the most, and why that one?

2. The Bible tells us who we really are: *royalty*, created in the image of God our King. Why can it be hard for us to believe, really believe, in our God-given dignity? What are the opposite messages coming at us from this world?

3. Religion tells us to do better and try harder and pedal faster. In your life, what are examples of when you've attempted to change yourself with this mindset? *Why* doesn't this bring about the change we most deeply need?

4. As we dare to believe in our true identity, defined for us by God himself, what are some positive differences that awareness of this can make in us?

_____

_____

_____

_____

_____

5. What aspect of who Jesus is and what he did for us was most encouraging to you?

_____

_____

_____

_____

_____

_____

_____

———

Prayer

Father, thank you for giving me a royal identity and noble purpose. I confess that I have trivialized you and your calling on my life. I've been enslaved to sin and am unable to clean up the mess I've made. Thank you for sending Jesus to forgive and renew me. I receive your welcome. I trust your heart of love for me. I'm open to your renewing work to redeem every part of my heart and life. Thank you for giving me this hope. In Jesus's royal name. Amen.

LETTER 2

She Is Royalty

Chapter Summary

Every woman on a porn site matters more than we know. She is real, she is precious, and she is just as royal as you are. We are called to see her as God sees her and to defend her instead of abuse her. Every woman is just as much created in God's image as every man and therefore is worthy of the same respect. The beginning of the Bible shows Adam celebrating the dignity of Eve, and the end of the Bible shows that every redeemed woman will stand in awe-inspiring glory. We are called to respect every woman as a potential Queen of the New Creation.

This means every woman's sexuality is a sacred gift from God. Sexualized thoughts about a woman you are not married to is a violation of her sacredness. Satan *hates* women, and through porn Satan recruits millions of men to participate in assaulting, degrading, and denying women their true dignity. To look at porn is to side with Satan against both women and God. But God is calling us men to freedom—to a complete turnaround—which begins with *honesty*. God is calling us to be honest with ourselves about what is really happening and what we are really supporting when we look at porn. This is the key insight we're called to accept: "*Every* relationship is either Christlike or predatory."

Texts for Meditation and Memorization

Genesis 1:27

> God created man in his own image,
>   in the image of God he created him;
>   male and female he created them.

Matthew 5:27–28

> You have heard that it was said, "You shall not commit adultery."
> But I say to you that everyone who looks at a woman with lustful
> intent has already committed adultery with her in his heart.

———

Questions for Reflection and Discussion

1. As you read the second letter, what one insight stood out to you the most, and why that one?

_____

_____

_____

_____

_____

_____

2. The Bible gives us a vision of every woman's potential glory as a Queen of the New Creation. How can this insight—as you believe it deeply, moment by moment—change how you perceive and relate to women?

_____

_____

_____

_____

_____

3. The porn industry sure doesn't see women as royalty! What is this horrible industry saying to women about themselves? What is it saying to *us* about women—and about ourselves?

4. This second letter calls us to trade nice-sounding hypocritical words for straightforward and honest confessions about what we're really doing if we look at porn. What difference does it make when we start thinking this way, praying this way, and talking this way—with blunt honesty?

5. As the Bible opens our eyes to the God-given glory that every woman possesses, how does that biblical vision also dignify us men as we relate to women—whether online or in real life?

Prayer

Father, I praise you for making every woman in your royal image. Thank you for writing history in such a way that the new creation will be a world where redeemed women will stand in glory to reign with Christ. I confess that I have failed to see women as you see them. I have failed to treat them with the respect you say they deserve. Forgive me and help me to be honest about my sins. I want to grow in treating every woman in a Christlike way—in my heart and with my behavior. I pray this in the name of Jesus. Amen.

He Is Royalty

Chapter Summary

Jesus—the real Jesus—matters. And he cares about you and every woman. The real Jesus is different from the common false Jesuses on the market today. The "Feel-Good Jesus" says sexual sin is no big deal, and everyone will go to heaven, because everyone is basically good. The "Feel-Bad Jesus" always embarrasses you with your short-comings, and says you'll make it to heaven—if you measure up. But the *real* Jesus is surprisingly different. The real Jesus attracted moral failures and befriended them. He is grander than we think. He is both a conquering Lion and a slain Lamb. He is both the majestic and fearless King and the atoning sacrifice for our sins. He respects us enough to confront our sins, and he loves us enough to pay for our sins. This Jesus, the real Jesus, is enough for all our real need. In stark contrast, porn offers us endless hyperarousals, but it ultimately leaves us with the letdown of emptiness and self-hatred.

The choice before you is not between your normal life and a re-ligious life—with church on Sundays. The choice is between two worlds—the world dominated by Satan versus the new world being re-created by Jesus. In the first world, porn offers to turbocharge our sexuality, but it destroys our sexuality—and our freedom as serious men. In the new world, Jesus is gathering up exhausted sinners like us and giving them new life. For everyone in his new world, Jesus will return to renew the earth and make it sparkle forever.

Texts for Meditation and Memorization

Revelation 5:5–6

And one of the elders said to me, "Weep no more; behold, the Lion of the tribe of Judah, the Root of David, has conquered, so that he can open the scroll and its seven seals."

And between the throne and the four living creatures and among the elders I saw a Lamb standing, as though it had been slain, with seven horns and with seven eyes, which are the seven spirits of God sent out into all the earth.

Colossians 1:13–14

He has delivered us from the domain of darkness and transferred us to the kingdom of his beloved Son, in whom we have redemption, the forgiveness of sins.

―

Questions for Reflection and Discussion

1. As you read the third letter, what one insight stood out to you the most, and why that one?

2. Two common false Jesuses are the "Feel-Good Jesus" and the "Feel-Bad Jesus." Which one of these tends to sneak into your own mind in the moments leading up to sin? How would believing in and relating to the real Jesus help you in those moments?

3. "Every time you log on to a porn site, what you're really looking for is Jesus." What do you think about that statement? If it's true, then how is every porn site lying to us, tricking us with its false "salvation"?

4. Lust and porn make men feel powerful in the moment. But how does it end up robbing us of authority and freedom?

5. If your own guilty conscience ever tells you that Jesus probably hates you, so there's no hope and you might as well give in to porn, how does this letter empower you to defy that despair and keep fighting for your integrity?

Prayer

Lord Jesus, I praise you for being both the Lion from the tribe of Judah and the Lamb who was slain for our sins. You are far better than any of our self-invented versions of you. You are both more serious about sin and more gracious toward sinners than we would expect. I confess that I have sinned because I have not respected your kingship. And I've often hidden in shame and not come to you afterward because I have not believed in your grace. Thank you for opening up to me your new world of freedom and grace. Count me in! I honor you as my truest friend and eagerly await your return to make all things new. I pray this in your holy name, Jesus. Amen.

PART 2

REIMAGINING
THE FUTURE

LETTER 4

We Can Do This

Chapter Summary

You have a royal identity and purpose. So the question for you now is *What are you going to do with it?* Your stature is not for you alone but for you to liberate others. You can stand as a prophetic presence in our world, making bold new moves with historic impact. God is like a divine Coach who has put you in the game, and it's time to start running his plays. Our moment in history is like the final months of World War II, between D-Day and VE-Day: Jesus has already won the decisive battle in his death and resurrection, and the end of the war is now inevitable. We aren't fighting *for* victory but *in* victory.

We can get ready for our personal fight with three steps. First, know what you're fighting for. Jesus is a noble man who makes noble plans, and he will call us to stand only for noble things. True nobility is not about doing the bare minimum but about generously volunteering to do all that's best for others. Second, know how you can fight well. You can fight well by guarding your own heart from both lustful thoughts and despairing thoughts. Third, know what winning will cost you. With Jesus's help, you must *kill* the sin that is keeping you from whole-heartedly following him. The soldiers of Jesus don't kill others. They put to death the predatory impulses within themselves.

Texts for Meditation and Memorization

Isaiah 32:8

> But he who is noble plans noble things,
> and on noble things he stands.

Proverbs 4:23

> Keep your heart with all vigilance,
> for from it flow the springs of life.

———

Questions for Reflection and Discussion

1. As you read the fourth letter, what one insight stood out to you the most, and why that one?

2. One key step in our fight against sin is *guarding* our hearts. Very practically, what can this look like in the moment when you are strongly tempted to commit sexual sin?

3. Despair strengthens porn, and hope strengthens integrity. What are practical ways you, together with your friends, can keep the hope of the gospel alive in your heart day by day?

4. This letter said, "I know of only one thing harder than obeying the Lord, and that is *not* obeying the Lord." What does this mean, in your own words? From your own life, what is an example of where you have found not obeying the Lord to be hard, painful, costly?

5. If porn is like that lizard on the man's shoulder, whispering lies in his ear, what lies does the lizard whisper to your heart? And what if the Holy Spirit kills that lizard? It would be scary, but what might you gain by opening up to God that radically?

Prayer

Father, thank you for accomplishing a great and decisive victory over sin, death, and Satan through Jesus's death and resurrection. I receive your call to enter the battle, and I'm willing to follow you. Please give me the strength to fight against lustful impulses. And if I fail, give me the strength not to despair but to keep bringing myself back to you. Thank you for creating my sexuality. I devote it to you now and for the rest of my days—for your noble purposes. I pray this in the name of Jesus. Amen.

We Can Work Together

Chapter Summary

Your integrity cannot grow and flourish if you go it alone. In order to make your life count, you *must* participate in honest brotherhood. Our problem is not merely individual but cultural. Our world has become a culture of abuse. This is why we need a counterculture of integrity. We will get traction as we gather other men to experience together a new kind of community—deep belonging and gentle safety.

The key scripture to guide us into this new brotherhood is James 5:16: "Therefore, confess your sins to one another and pray for one another, that you may be healed." Three realities stand out. First, confession. We overcome our sins not by heroic willpower but through confession. At least one other man *must* know what you're really facing deep inside you. Second, prayer. Prayer doesn't seem powerful to us, but it's a powerful way God works in our lives. And what counts is not your eloquence but your honesty. Third, healing. God answers our prayers with healing—not just physical healing but also the spiritual healing of *felt* forgiveness. As you meet with a brother one-on-one, you can also begin including others in a new community of confession, prayer, and deep healing.

Texts for Meditation and Memorization

James 5:16

> Therefore, confess your sins to one another and pray for one another, that you may be healed.

Isaiah 57:15

> For thus says the One who is high and lifted up,
>   who inhabits eternity, whose name is Holy:
> "I dwell in the high and holy place,
>   and also with him who is of a contrite and lowly spirit,
> to revive the spirit of the lowly,
>   and to revive the heart of the contrite."

Questions for Reflection and Discussion

1. As you read the fifth letter, what one insight stood out to you the most, and why that one?

2. In what unhealthy or unhelpful way have you tried to change yourself or practice "accountability" in the past? How does the vision of brotherhood in this letter give you a more realistic and hopeful pathway for transformation?

3. "Son, you can be impressive, or you can be known, but you can't be both." Who are the trustworthy men in your area with whom you can be less impressive and more known?

4. This letter offers some verses from the Bible: Philippians 1:27, Isaiah 57:15, Luke 4:18, and James 5:16–17. This letter also quotes some great Christian men: Ray Ortlund Sr., Dietrich Bonhoeffer, and Martin Luther. Which verse or quotation might serve you best as a positive rallying point for gathering more men together in honest brotherhood?

5. What is the next step you want to take in light of this letter, and what is your plan for taking that step?

———

Prayer

Father in heaven, I praise and honor you as the One who is high and lifted up and whose name is Holy. Thank you that you dwell not just in the high and holy place but also down here with the lowly. You promise to dwell with those who have messed up and who look to you alone for healing. Help me face the evil of pornography honestly. Give me courage to confess my sins openly to you and to a brother. Bring the healing that only you can give. And for your own sake and the good of so many other brothers and sisters, use me, in my weakness, to grow a counterculture of true brotherhood. In Jesus's name. Amen.

We Can Make a World of Difference

Chapter Summary

We live in days of exceptional evil, calling us to exceptional good, no matter the cost. Jesus is building a world of nobility, and his plan is to build it through you and me—men of integrity. As our world gets increasingly dark, God will help us to spread his light. This letter offers a number of practical strategies. They may not be impressive, but they are surprisingly powerful.

First, stay on the anvil. Be a man of *growing* integrity. No matter how hard God's hammer falls, he will reshape you into the kind of man you long to be. Second, tell your story. Take time to write down a short and simple narrative of the way God is helping you grow. You will be ready to help a friend understand how God can do the same for him. Third, pray. Prayer is powerful, because God is powerful. Pray before, during, and after everything you do, and God will enter into everything you do. Fourth, get married. Unless Jesus calls you to serve as a single man, fall in love with a woman who loves Jesus, and enjoy your imperfect but amazing marriage. Fifth, create. Culture changes through art. You can fight against porn, and for justice, through the weapons of art—like music, novels, movies, and so forth. Sixth, advocate. One of the greatest ways to trigger social change is to go public with your own experience of healing. Seventh, rejoice. Resolve to replace self-pity with rejoicing in the Lord. Joy prevails over evil with unstoppable power.

Texts for Meditation and Memorization

2 Timothy 2:21

> Therefore, if anyone cleanses himself from what is dishonorable, he will be a vessel for honorable use, set apart as holy, useful to the master of the house, ready for every good work.

Philippians 2:12–13

> Therefore, my beloved, as you have always obeyed, so now, not only as in my presence but much more in my absence, work out your own salvation with fear and trembling, for it is God who works in you, both to will and to work for his good pleasure.

Questions for Reflection and Discussion

1. As you read the sixth letter, what one insight stood out to you the most, and why that one?

2. One strategy this letter commends is telling your own story—a short and simple narrative of how God is helping you. What are the key elements of that short narrative for you?

3. Culture changes through creative people using their songs, stories, films, and so forth for lament, protest, courage, and joy. What creative gifts do you have that can be used for this noble cause of spreading light in darkness? Do you have a brother in Christ who has unique creative gifts whom you could encourage for this cause?

4. What is one risk the Lord is now calling you to take to help build a world where more people are treated with dignity? His plan for you will include small steps. But every positive new step helps. What is *your* next step—even if it does feel risky?

5. The sixth letter concludes by fast-forwarding to your final day in this world. When you come to that day and you're looking back on your life journey, what will thrill you then? What will grieve you then? So, what bold changes must you make today?

Prayer

Father, thank you for inviting me into your plan to build a world of nobility. I love that your plan to change the world includes unleashing your power through weak men like me. I don't deserve to be a part of this, and so I praise you for not only forgiving me but also enlisting me for your cause. Help me become a man of integrity. Help me become a man of prayer. Help me become a man of risk-taking courage. Give me insight into what next steps would be wisest for me to take. And give me the compassion to take these steps. I need you. But I also have you. Thank you. In Jesus's holy name. Amen.